# Skipping Stones on the River Styx

*poems by*

# Elizabeth Rae Bullmer

*Finishing Line Press*
Georgetown, Kentucky

# Skipping Stones on the River Styx

## ACKNOWLEDGMENTS

Thank you to the following publications for first featuring these poems.

"Let Me Explain the Grieving Process," Poetry Society of Michigan, *Peninsula Poets Contest Edition*
"Instructions for Midwinter Surrender," *Pensive: A Global Journal for Spirituality & the Arts* (issue 7 )
"Visitor," *The Paddock Review*

Publisher: Leah Huete de Maines
Editor: Christen Kincaid
Cover Art: Devin Bullmer
Author Photo: Robin Church
Cover Design: Elizabeth Maines McCleavy


Order online: www.finishinglinepress.com
also available on amazon.com

Author inquiries and mail orders:
Finishing Line Press
PO Box 1626
Georgetown, Kentucky 40324
USA

# Contents

# The Mathematics of Loss

If I was 22 & 27 when I birthed my children
and their father died at 39,
how long will both my children live?

If I was 14 & 19 both times my father died
and my children were 13 & 19 when their father died;
if my grandmother lived to 95, but I will never be a grandmother,
how long will I live as their mother?

My father was born in St. Louis in 1923,
my mother was born in Delaware in 1947,
and I was born in Kalamazoo in 1976.
How far and at what speed does Love travel?

My grandmother arrived on the 2nd day of the 1st month
of a Gregorian year, my mother arrived 20 years + 8 months later
on a midsummer day marked 2,
and her grandson arrived at the cusp of reason & emotion
on a 22, the same month, 57 years later.
Measure the distance between their perspectives, by degrees,
and calculate the point of intersection.

and her grandson arrived at the cusp of reason & emotion
on a 22, the same month, 57 years later.
Measure the distance between their perspectives, by degrees,
and calculate the point of intersection.

My daughter & I were both born on days marked 17,
22 years + 6 months apart, unspecified degrees
from opposing equinoxes.
If they now live in Berlin while I remain in the United States,
how many nautical miles must we each swim to meet halfway?

My husband & his father were both born in spring,
between vacillating new moons and Easters.
If both died on days marked 13, 4 years + 8 months apart,
one on a Sunday evening at home, one alone
on a Monday morning before first birds,
when and where will they meet again?

If my father would have lived 100 years next autumn
but died 27 years ago on Samhain,
how many more years must I light a candle
to guide his passage home?

If it's been 33 years since my first loss
and 13 + 31 + 13 days since my latest,
how long does it take memory's mass
to exceed the density of emptiness?

## Ghost Beads

The farther you drift beyond
the Bardos, Saturn's bracelets
luring you home,
the more disparate your face—
pixels pixelating into empty
space within a shell of sky.

I chew on my memory of you
like an ant eating
the interior of a juniper berry—
grinding until it's gone.
I lift the hollow orb,
holding what I thought I knew
of you, us, life.

I breathe into it all I can
remember, to string like popcorn
at Christmas, to wrap
around the trunk of my throat.

This is how you hold me now.

## How We Hold On

If my hands were birds    I would cease to believe in cages
fear the sting of clipped wings    if your voice
were a siren song    I would cease to imagine free will
surrender at the feet of Fate    I come from people
who shunned god    while claiming the moral majority
you come from people    who drank and smoked their faith
to death    we come from people who break bones of birds
to make wishes    cast like fountain pennies into the Void
people who never learned how to sing    what drums do we have
to gather us home?    what stories worth weaving into rugs
for our children to kneel in prayer?    if your heart were a bonfire
I would dance circles around it    and my feet would make drums
of the Earth's own skin    if my breath were wind    I would
lift the glowing embers of all your desire to heaven    for angels
to gather    rather than toss away    if our love were water
it would wash shame clean    and children would never again
need to pray    if your voice were a siren song    I would follow it
over the cliffs of knowing    if my hands were birds
I would set them free    and I would see    I would see
if they ever came back

## The Jinn

Sits tight indefinitely. Squeezes their metaphorical knees to
their hypothetical chest and contemplates the nature of longing.
Words and rewords requests, negotiating verbs and pronouns,
flipping through a deck of adjectives. They begin with common causes:
health, death, peace, love, and all the side streets—reciprocation,
protection, vindication, revenge. Then they go to work on more
aggressive demands: power, prowess, possession—all that may be
possessed. Few ask for the ephemeral: happiness, hope, harmony,
but the Jinn consider these anyway; there's plenty of time,
if time exists at all in this liminal field of infinite possibility,
chained to the dogged predictability of human desire.

If I decide to rub the lamp, dubiously stroke its dusty, silvered spine—
and I'm not saying that I will—do not expect me to join you,
however enticing your endlessness. If it meant your immediate return
to this walking world, I would not set you free.

## Grief Is a Terrible Housemate

It never scrapes a plate.
Piles sauce-crusted pans
in the sink. Leaves socks
on countertops and couches.
Uses my toothbrush
without apology. Puts empty
boxes back on shelves. Never
turns off the television. Eats
all my groceries. Buys wine
when I say I'm done drinking.
Presses chocolate against
my tongue when I'm finished
with sweetness. Seduces
my heartache in front of me.
Laughs at its heartbroken
jokes. Rubs its shoulders
and offers to bake cookies.
This is not a kindness. These
subtleties are thinly veiled
viciousness. I haven't missed
that mean glint, jealous snarl.
I know it waits until I fall asleep
to read my diary. Leans its blanched
lips close. Whispers horror into my ears.

## Six-Year Somniloquy

You spoke only static—
audible lint between call signs.
You must have crushed tissue
paper into my pillow
while I slept, spread shadow-
puppet panoramas over walls;
we never established a code.

Your negative space needed to touch
everything, like a criminal hoping for capture.
Dark-matter fingerprints devouring furniture,
walls, doorknobs, threatening, *You're next.*

There was a period of toddler
tantrums, knocking knickknacks
from tables, banging piano keys,
shoving books from shelves
to fall open on the floor—
I stuffed my ears with socks
to staunch your wailing.

Once you realized you could not return,
that I would not soon join you in that dark,
the absence of you chilled the air.
Silence is what surrounds me now.

I fold it like laundry, bathe it
as my child, humming the dirge
you once sang when we danced
in the living room, as if we were
lovers. I tell it bedtime stories,
tuck it under covers beside me
and kiss it goodnight.

## Let Me Explain the Grieving Process

I used to have a husband        or—I have eight
table saws        or—a tangle of bungee cords or—
I have a plate        full of rings        that used to be
friends        like—once my grandmother was
a gold perfume jar        or—beautiful
turquoise bead        now lost        I mean—
I wore the same pendant        every day
for years        a rune        with my father's name
like—I used to wear his puka shells
from Guam        or—I used to wear his dog tags
or—when my father-in-law died        all I wanted
was my dad's worry stone back        like—
I give away everything sacred


or—I've run out of ways to tell you        I'm lonely
I mean—devastated        I mean—two people drowned
in their own car        in a puddle        under an overpass
like—they just drove into a flood        or—the flood
became a whale and swallowed them        or—
some days are the color of tornado        like—
the whole world has been broken        by wind
like—everything will land        miles from its home
or—everything is made of sand        like—I'm a sandcastle
I mean—that is how it tastes        or—maybe
I've seen too many dead people        dove-belly grey
or—white-ashen eyes        or—bloated plums
sprouting from mouths        like—in Dachau
we saw photographs        piles of human bodies
I don't even know how many        I mean—
barely bones        I mean—that        is the way it feels

## The Day I Die

I wonder, will it feel different
right away, waking with a gasp?
A flower petal's last grasp at color
before the faded fall. Will I notice
a swift slice of wind, icy wraith
slipping down the shaft of my spine,
lifting every inch of skin—a shiver
in sunshine? Perhaps nature will

sense my imminent end, trees
extending limbs for a final embrace.
The cats clamor and crowd against me
with wide, imploring eyes, incessant
meows, warning. Or will everything
sing of memory and family:
series of emergency flares out-
lining a highway crash site

in the dim trickery of dusk?
Display of Ginsberg and Kerouac,
borrowed books I never returned;
screaming shelves of my dead
husband's belongings I have yet
to let go. Stranger smoking a cigarette
wears Dad's square, goldenrod smile.
Whiff of Nana's ancient perfume—

the gold-clasped container, sky-blue
enamel bead. Seashell collection
in a narrow glass jar. Must I feel
compelled to call my sister?
Invite my children to lunch, kiss
all over their faces, as I once did
when bedtime was the best time of day—
singing and stories, shadow puppets?

They begged me to linger, longing
for only a few minutes more
before cascading into the mind's
liminal wonderland. Will I too plead
for one more lullaby, last slow
dance with my lover? Will I stand
at the indifferent edge of that long
deep, swaying, blinking back sleep,
still terrified to be left alone

in the dark? Will it come sudden,
stricken, urgent heart flicking:
faces, foods, favorite poems, pain,
rainstorms, sacred places, laughter,
love songs, loss, unthinkable bliss.
Blessings flashed in quick succession
before the reel's expected, yet somehow

shocking end—black and white
numbers, gush of static: ocean
speaking its deepest passion to the wind,
a mechanical beep, and darkness descends.

## Loss Knows Only One Name

It is never what we think it is.

We climb the mountains we have
made in our own backyards

as if god itself scraped them
from the landscape. We sit cross-legged,

with hope perched like a sparrow
on our shoulder. Soon she will be

a hawk scanning for subtlety, then
an owl hunting down our dreams.

We will stay beyond the sunset and moon-
rise, wait for stars to answer our prayers.

The rustle of every leaf speaks last
words, parroting all we have lost—

we want to answer back to the frigid
wind, we want to bind our words to

stone, smooth as polished jasper.
We would keep it in our pocket, always

searching for a stranger with feathers
in their eyes. Without thinking,

we would reach out and press it
into their desperately empty palm; pass it

like a note from a former self saying,
*Keep it close to you. Keep it safe.*

## Invitation

Who:   Widow dressed in white
collecting cardinal feathers
like notes passed by the dead,
a papier mâché corpse.

What:   Occasion marked only
after the fact. Hollow cake
with elaborate icing. Sinkhole,
unexpected swallowing
of once seemingly solid ground.

When:   Every year, as the weather turns
to face the last corner of autumn—
fallen leaves, glitter-bombed
by frost.

Where:   Garage-shaped piñata packed
with stacked wood and broken hand-
tools dangling precariously
in the ghostly wash of a bare
fluorescent bulb.

Why:   Loss is the chrysalis
we struggle inside
to strengthen our wings.

How:   Open your eyes, open
your hands, open
your mouth and release the bees
collected in your heart.

## 52 Hertz

it is a bullet embedded
in the body—no exit
wound—tarnishing tissue

the gutted hollow
of a split-open peach pit

perpetually swallowing
the floating
bone in our throat

it is the frequency of grief
barely
audible to human ears

forever tribeless

the mournful moan roaming
alone
at the bottom of the sea

submarines search endlessly
combing the depths
we dare    but some

sadness stays
unable
or unwilling to surface

## Polaris

The brightest star in the northern night sky,
flickering tip of the Little Bear's tail,
guiding sailors and survivors home,
cannot be seen at all from below the sash
of equator cinching Earth to her orbit.

And those who rely so completely
on this North Star to navigate their way
will never see the Southern Cross
nor Southern Crown. I can see Venus
shimmering beyond the unblinking eye
of the moon, from the end of my driveway

in Michigan. On a clear night, in hunting season,
I will find Orion's belt. I will point and name,
and for a moment I will believe
that naming means knowing a thing at all.

## Diagnosis

we don't have to name everything      like the space
between two mouths sharing intimate stories      there are
places to inhabit      so small      if we lose sight
for even an instant      we may never call it *home* again
I wanted to live there with you      to understand
every flicker of lip      speak in code      raised eyebrows
flared nostrils      wanted to know your secret
handshake      keep your spare key      rescue you
when you were stranded      if there were a deserted island
and you were on it      I wanted to be there too      at first
basking under the emphatic sun      perhaps even there
you would have found a cave to seek shelter      somewhere
deep and cool      if I had known      what to look for
tracked your footprints      followed you into that hole
convinced you to return to shore      build sandcastles
at low tide      knowing we would do it again tomorrow
it could have been delightful      no agenda      to soothe
your anxiety      to quell that plea for approval
we could have removed our clothes      sewn an enormous flag
to wave at god      naked as Eve      until the end

## I Sing to Dead People

usually naked, my torso smooth
shellacked skin of box-harp
strings soft as cherub's cheek

pluck and twang language
less literal than my own
speaking ancestral connection:

the still-oscillating bones
of dead elephants, passed
from trunk to trunk

trying to understand loss
as a dance for the living
the tremulous echo of all

that was, forever filling
the space between us,
caressing us always:

the singular note vibrating
from the throat of each
star in the universe

## If I told you I swallowed the moon

and all that remained of her glow
was an echo
           emanating
from the hollow of my open mouth
           breathing
beams back to the heavens,
her golden silhouette
           gilding
my holy throat, would you still

love me, the way sand loves water,
even if she draws it away from land
only to blow it
into the deep-dark unknown?

Would you love the pull of my womb,
           aching—
the moon's bright edge
           bulging
in my belly, the ebb and flow of wounds
           healing, reopening
like petals perpetually puffing pollen
only to fade in the fall—the way

night takes us all, eventually,
with or without a guiding light?

If I told you I was that compass,
you just had to trust me,
if I promised I knew the path,
would you follow me all the way home?

## How I Define Reality

As the light returns to the land, a sliver
        more each morning, my days seem
a vast emptiness, like urban streets at 4 a.m.,
        speaking the mechanical language of
cell phone towers and fluorescent lights.

How can I remain so solid, so sure—
        the earth in my bones sewn into skin
by gravity's thread, binding me to sunrise
        and sunset, compelling me to count
moons and number my years?

I might think my life is a cluster of last
        summer's wild berries, shriveled
on brittle vines, unusually exposed, this still-
        green winter. Then I close my eyes
and there is more: the staircase within a willow;

cool aqua-colored cave; winged horse
        in an abandoned white-stone city;
the forest where I dance with ancestors, dressed
        as birds of prey; trees full of foreign fruits,
their seeds a timeless realm of stars.

## What I Have Not Named

chartreuse-rimmed gaze of an upright cat
tail curled like a tongue
around an unasked question

the odd shape of my smallest toe

amputation scars on tree trunks
all the lost limbs

discovery of animal bones in the woods—
antler, rabbit jaw, rodent pelvis—
like a love note from god

irony of collecting things that decompose

keeping the clothes of dead relatives
though they do not fit

how the body tightens with grief

that voracious longing of the soul

rapid flutter of brittle leaves across the yard
which could be a flock of grounded brown birds
or a posse of small squirrels
or an omen

the understanding that at any moment
despite all of this
god could open their irresistible mouth
and exhale

## The Dying Process

### I.

when it started:
the moment i was born.
first time i heard a bird
fly full force into a window.
first time i peeled a stiff
dried earthworm from pavement.
perhaps even now i am
slowly disintegrating—
a stone broken by ocean.

### II.

one morning, on vacation
500 miles from home
i found a bug crawling
in the bathroom sink.

that evening, the same bug
lay dead on the floor
beside the toilet.
its entire last day's
journey spanned a distance
of less than four feet.

### III.

if i grieve it all now
will it hurt less later?
the ache of loving you,
our impending goodbye.

i lower my voice, memorize
your breath, follow
the fine lines of your face
into each new expression.

i see you completely. know
you completely. i am
you. you are me.
this is the dying process.

IV.

i can only now see it
for what it is—beginning
inside of an end. i have been
a student of Death all my life:
seen it come slowly as sunset's
subtle green wink before dusk.
watched it linger—shriveled
leaf refusing to fall. sicken
and suffer like soft fruit
left too long on the vine. seen it
sudden as summer thunder
cracks a robin's egg sky.
i have held it in my hands.
in my mouth. the way
a mother carries her young.
i have swallowed the fear of it
so i would not see it stalking.
so it could not look me in the eyes.

## Skipping Stones on the River Styx

*One.*

For Nana, a seashell, orange and
white gnarled arthritic finger pointing,
brittle lump of calcified knucklebones.
Or a strand of pearls plucked one by one
—they almost make it across.

*Two.*

For Grandpa—a fistful of rocks.

*Three.*

National Enquirer, folded into boat form,
sets sail on the steel-black surface.
Unwrapped candies, lurid red and gold,
melt into the slow molten wake:
final sunset Grandma never saw.

*Four.*

Pop-pop, I whisper gratitudes into whirling
eddies. Echoes of your shared stories
leave faint footprints on the water.

*Five.*

Dad, dare I drown the worry stone I gave
you to compete with the memory of another
little girl you'd carried since the war?
*It's all I have left.*

*Six. Seven.*

Renato.

Jason.

*Eight. Nine.*

Maarten.

Kristin.

*Ten.*

Kisses for Cass.
Blown clear to the other side.
*Collect them.*

*Eleven.*

A copy of *Howl.* Sliver of purpleheart
wood. Antique hammer.
Silver finishing nail slaps ashore.

*Twelve.*     A blank Scrabble tile for Mom-mom
              buoyantly bounds. The Q. The Z.

*Thirteen.*   Joe, if I toss you the compass you gave
              to your son—bronze disc
              whisking over ebony mist—
              will you give it to him once again?
              *May it help him find his way.*

## Visitor

I must remember to say
thank you. Must wipe feet
by the door, close it
behind me. Must not forget
where I came from,
must someday follow
the tamped ashes of ancestors,
travelers all. Must go
the way I came. Innocent
me once more. Hollow
me, body of bone, bamboo,
sunflower stalk. Flute me.
Tune me to the key
of a baby's delighted squeal.

Remember the songs
I sang to children. Thump of drums
in my chest. How similar the longing
of love and loss. Grief me again
and again. Ecstatic tomatoes split
open on the vine. Tumultuous
tang of homemade pickles.
Honor the sacrificial sting
of a honeybee. Thick, golden-sweet.
Amber me. Mosquito me.

Naked me. Offering of skin
burning bare against my belly.
Euphoric swell crashing ashore.
Must climb trees, braid baskets
from yellow-green willow wands.
Must ride bicycles into the wind.
Dance me. Music me. Pelt me
like overfed raindrops into
malnourished dirt. Vacant lakebeds.
Must not forget what remains
as I slip back into the dark.
Gap me. Elysian Field me.
Must appreciate all of this
when I am gone.

## Instructions for Midwinter Surrender

Let the cat climb the window. Let her drag her wet
pink nose across the glass in thin white streaks.

Let the fox squirrel steal pepitas from the red squirrel.
Let the expired Christmas tree decompose on the porch.

Let snow. Let frigid. Let dust make itself seen.
Let Isis spread her wings and Ganesha's thick dance.

Let god answer the prayers of others. Let others.
Let inhale and exhale. Let lungs and liver. Let heart.

Let the piano remain unplayed. Let cello. Let violin.
Let guitar in its ancient case. Let hand-drum and harp.

Let stray cat fur construct another cat in the crevice
of the couch. Let the collection of wooden chopsticks.

Let books and books and books. Let words weave
worlds away. Let manifest dreams. Let childhood

innocence—like unborn flowers fantasizing bees,
like earthworms sung to sleep by deep mycelium.

Let it be easy. These rigid hands, this clamped mouth,
let them open as the sky's windblown throat

before rain. Let the air grow bloated, full
as a belly before birthing. A birthday balloon.

Let joy. Let love with her carnival-glass eyes.
Her confetti eruptions. Let loose. Let it free memory—

the iridescent sheath, distant and shiny before expiring,
becoming the space we breathe in. The space we breathe out.

**Elizabeth Rae Bullmer** has been writing since the age of seven. She received her B.A. in Theatre and English, with Emphasis in Creative Writing and Performance, from Alma College. For over twenty years, Elizabeth has taught writing workshops for all ages of students and adults, she has participated in Western Michigan University's Peace Jam and competed nationally as a performance poet on two Kalamazoo Slam teams, as well as placing ninth at the 2004 individual World Poetry Slam. Her many hobbies include knitting, painting, cooking, all manner of kitchen science and she suspects herself to be an undiagnosed bibliophile. She shares her home with four extremely demanding felines and her two phenomenal, adult children are her top role models. Elizabeth works as a self-employed, licensed massage and sound therapist in Kalamazoo, MI, where she actively serves on multiple community arts boards. *Skipping Stones on the River Styx* is her fifth chapbook.